FIRST DAY

FIRST DAYS

First Days: How to build a therapy business and stay sane

By Ann Jaloba HPD, MNCH (Acc), Dip.HPsych, Cert.SM, Dip.NLP

ISBN-13:
978-1493736348

ISBN-10:
1493736345

Published by Helping Handbooks Publishing, 26 Tapton Mount Close Sheffield S10 5DJ

DEDICATION

To all my clients, who have taught me more than they know

FIRST DAYS

ABOUT THE AUTHOR

Ann Jaloba works as a hypnotherapist in Sheffield where she has been running a busy practice for five years. She edits The Hypnotherapy Journal, the journal of the National Council for Hypnotherapy (the largest not for profit hypnotherapy organisation in the UK). Ann also works as a trainer, mentor and supervisor for other therapists and is the author of several training manuals and skills books. You can find out more by visiting www.wellthought.co.uk

FIRST DAYS

CONTENTS

FOREWORD

This is an excellent practical primer and how-to book for therapists setting up a private practice using hypnosis. The book is designed for practitioners in the UK. The 11 chapters build on each other as the subject develops. There are sufficient details covering all aspects of a private practice so that the book serves as a check-list for things to do and take care of.

There is a significant emphasis on marketing a beginning practice, and this is as it should be. How do you get started and get a sufficient number of clients for the practice to be viable and sustaining? How should your office be furnished and arranged? What materials should you have available to give to clients? How do you talk with clients on the phone when they are inquiring about a first session? What is your fee structure, and how do you communicate that to your clients in a straightforward and reasonable way? What do you do about no-shows and clients who cancel at short notice? When your schedule is not full, what do you do with the "spare" time? Is it okay to communicate with your clients by phone? Email? Texting? Social media? How do you limit phone conversations when you have a session coming up? What kinds of records should you keep? Is giving homework part of your practice? Does it make sense to have clients pre-pay for a given number of sessions? What about doing pro bono work or giving talks to local groups? How do you handle "difficult" clients, and how do you develop or find "golden" clients?

The above practical questions (and many more) are answered in this book for the beginner. It will be your guide to a successful practice, and has been written by someone who has struggled with these questions to build her own private practice. In fact, this book itself will be your first investment in your future.

Rubin Battino, MS
2014
Yellow Springs, Ohio, USA

FIRST DAYS

Introduction

I began working as a hypnotherapist in 2009. At first I had no clients at all, yet within a year I was working full time. Getting busier was great. I had been determined to make a success of my new career and now everything was turning out as I had hoped.

I learned more in this year than in any other year since before I started school at four and a half. And I made many mistakes. Luckily for me, none were disastrous (I don't think so anyway, perhaps something may come back to haunt me). Yet a couple of examples are still with me.

I will never forget that sinking feeling when two clients knocked on my door at the same time. In this instance, the mistake had been made by one of the clients, but it still felt awkward and she had travelled a long way to see me. At that point I decided to begin to send all my clients alerts by text the day before their appointment. I haven't counted how many times the client has replied telling me they had the wrong time, or they had forgotten, or they would have to cancel, but it is certainly enough to make that text worthwhile.

About the same time, I began to notice the filing cabinets and drawers in my office were getting fuller, and I was finding it harder and harder to lay my hands on materials I needed. I have never liked administrative tasks, and had been lucky enough in my corporate career to have some excellent personal assistants who kept me organised. I wasn't really in a financial position to pay an assistant at this stage, and anyway I decided it would take me longer to explain what I needed than to sort myself out. So, by trial and error, I devised a simple admin system which I hope can help you as well.

These are just a couple of examples from hundreds. Talk about a steep learning curve. Some of it was exciting and other times it was banging head on the desk time, yelling: "How could I have missed that."

By starting up a business you are risking making mistakes. The fail-safe way to avoid them is to do nothing, but that isn't going to build your business. So the answer is to mitigate the risks and try to avoid the mistakes. I hope this book will achieve that for you.

Setting up a business can be exhilarating, and it can be terrifying at the same time. Suddenly you are totally responsible for your workload, the quality of your work, your cash flow, legal aspects of your practice . . .and that is just for starters. A very famous therapist once told me that on leaving his full-time high-flying corporate career for the last time he felt a wave of terror. He put it this way: 'If I don't do something tomorrow, nothing will happen. I won't have clients, I won't have money.'

So it is down to you and that can be scary, but it can also be wonderfully exciting. Most of you will have made a deliberate choice to go into this future. You are almost certainly independent, resourceful and confident, optimistic and driven. So you have the qualities which are most important to successful self-employment.

Since my early days, I have given presentations to new therapists and I run one-to-one coaching sessions for people setting up new businesses. I came to realise that many of my errors were common and therapists newer than me were grateful to be able to learn from my mistakes.

So I wrote this book. It is worth saying that no-one noticed most of my mistakes, except me. When I had to 'fess up to a client they were almost always understanding and kind. A sincere apology and a sense of humour goes a long way. So don't be afraid of getting your business going in case you make a mistake. But if you would like to know how to avoid some of the more obvious ones, then keep on reading.

Ann Jaloba
www.firstdays.co.uk

Chapter One
What you have to have
Everything you need to do before the first client comes through the door.

You probably have an idea of how you would like your therapy space to be. But one word of warning, don't spend fortunes in money and time getting something you feel is perfect.

Much better to get started and then adapt and change as you learn what your clients want. What seems perfect and very important for you might not concern your clients that much. Having said that, you will be spending a lot of time in your room so make sure it feels a good fit for you.

If you are working from home check your lease and your insurance. Whether you are working from home, in a new office or as part of a therapy centre the things listed below are the minimum you will need. These are essential. If you are shown a room which doesn't have them, it is a deal breaker.

The essentials
• Is it clean?
• Is it tidy?
• Is the bell working? Can you turn the bell off (or not hear it) when you are in session?
• Is the temperature right: comfortable and controllable?
• Does the room feel private (can you be certain you will not be disturbed while in session)?

•If there is a telephone landline, can you turn it off?
•If there is a telephone landline, can it silently take messages?

Very important
• Are the chairs comfortable? Remember some of your clients may be overweight, in pain, or suffering from a degenerative disease. If you are a 25-year-old athlete then a chair you find comfortable and easy to get in and out of might not feel like that for those less fortunate. General rules: not too low, good supportive back, and arms on the chair to help the client to relax.
• Is it quiet? If not how are you going to deal with any ambient   noise   or distractions? ("White noise" as offered to people with tinnitus can be useful here.)
• Does the building have "kerb appeal"? A good-looking building can be a great marketing tool on your website. Conversely, a scruffy building will give out the wrong messages to your client.
• Is the entrance to the room clean, tidy, and welcoming?
• Is there sufficient parking? This is very important, and you might not realise it if you don't drive. A client who has had to drive around for minutes looking for a space is not going to arrive in a good state for therapy. City centres are an exception, but choose somewhere on good transport links.
• Is your room accessible to people with mobility problems? It may be you cannot offer full accessibility in which case you should say that in your publicity. However, you will see clients who are not fully mobile and don't tell you. So plan what you will do in this situation.

Travelling to a client's home
Many new therapists decide they will travel to a client's home as a way of building up their client base. It can be a great "extra" to offer, but take some basic security precautions and let a colleague or friend know where you are going and arrange to contact them to let them know you are safe when the

session is finished. Remember you are going to be in a situation where you do not control the environment. So you need to be doubly sure that you are safe and that it is an environment in which you can work. Here are some things to watch for.

If a client asks you to visit them, then check that they have the environment you need. Ask:

• Will you and the client will be alone in the house?
• Can you park easily?
• Do they have a quiet comfortable room?
• If there are kids around, where are they? Will they be quiet?
• Are there pets? Can they be kept quiet?

When you arrive ask:

• Is the telephone turned off/down?
• Would we be disturbed if someone rings the doorbell?
• Are they expecting any callers?
• If there are others in the house, do they know not to disturb the session?

Don't be isolated

You're running your own business and you've gained freedom. You can decide how you do things, who you see, what hours you work and how you structure your sessions and that feels wonderful.

On the downside, you are responsible for everything. That can be lonely. So what are you going to do when you hit a problem you can't solve? Who are you going to turn to when a session with a client goes badly?

This is where you will need a support network. Don't regard this as an optional extra. It is essential for your mental health and wellbeing.

So who is your support network?

Firstly, and at the top almost formal level, it might be a requirement of your professional registration to be in supervision. Spend time choosing your supervisor carefully; he or she will be the most important support you have. The supervisor is there to guide you, help you and make sure you are practising safely and to the best of your ability. You will, however be paying for this supervision and this may well mean you have to limit the time you spend with your supervisor.

So what other sources of support can you turn to? The first resource is yourself.

Do you keep a reflective diary? Many therapists do so while they are training and then stop. You will benefit by continuing to keep it, make it your friend, share your successes and your failures. There are different ways of keeping this diary. The one that works for me can be found at www.firstdays.co.uk but try out different formats until you find one that suits you. You may even decide to keep an audio diary. Whichever you choose, the act of recording your practice every day is a time to reflect, to unload and to let your feelings and emotions surface. As you build the diary up, you will find it is an invaluable record of how you felt, what you did, the ups and downs of your practice. It is an unequalled learning tool which will benefit you and your practise.

The next source of support is your peers. If you belong to a professional organisation, you may find it has an online forum or group where you can swap your experiences. Or you may be able to find a face-to-face peer group in your area; if not, perhaps you can set one up. The more local the better, being able to pop round for a coffee with someone on a slow day can be a lifeline.

Local business forums are sometimes useful to get support from other independent business people, as well as being able to talk about how it feels to be working for yourself. You may also pick up useful tips and contacts for services such as accountancy, marketing or web design.

You may be able to find a face-to-face peer group in your area; if not, perhaps you can set one up.

The people you trained with are another invaluable source of support. Many will be in a similar position to you as they begin their new career – and you know them already. This means you probably know who it's best to go to for a particular issue or problem. Perhaps you can set up a private Facebook page for your group?

How are you going to communicate with your clients?
Phones
You might want to consider getting a separate mobile phone just for your clients. That way you can switch it off when you are not working (with a message saying when you can call back of course). It means you can get a proper break, knowing that you can switch off completely.

If you are working from home, you might want to install a separate landline for the same reason, if you decide not to do this at the beginning then take care who answers the phone.

Sweet as they are, a six-year-old saying 'I'll get mummy,' is not the best start to a professional therapeutic relationship!

If you are going to be away from your phone a lot (perhaps you are only working part-time as a therapist) then it might be worth investing in a call answering service.

Some of these are run by virtual office companies and provide a professional reception service which will create a very good impression with new clients. Many of these companies will also provide you with other back up services such as business addresses. If you are working from home, you might not feel comfortable with having your home address all over the web so a business address might be worth thinking about.

Email
As with the phone, it is a good idea to set up a separate email address so you can keep your business and private life completely separate. Many website set-ups will include an email address and you can choose a name which reflects your business. My business is called Wellthought Talking Therapies and my email is ann@wellthought.co.uk.

There is one disadvantage to these web-based email systems: they are slower and lack the full functionality of applications such as Microsoft Outlook; so make sure you have the potential to upgrade when you get busy and have a bigger volume of web traffic to handle. I regularly remove client contact emails from my system and store them separately with password protection as an extra security measure to protect my clients.

Getting the information you need from clients
I set up a basic introduction page in my email folders to which I can just add the time and date of the client's appointment. (Go to www.firstdays.co.uk for an example, with explanatory notes on how to get the most out of the form and how to use it with clients). I find this a quick and easy way to make initial contact with my clients. This email also contains my basic information collection form, of which more later.

I often ask clients to print this off and bring it with them. It saves some time and gets them to commit to their treatment before they even step through the door, this sets up good habits and shows that you expect the client to take the treatment process seriously. However, some clients may be anxious, shy or lacking in confidence and in those cases it may be best to fill out the form face-to-face.

Professional services
I would strongly advise that you get an accountant from the outset; that means before a single client has paid you a single penny. An accountant will help you set up cash flow systems, balance sheets, profit and loss sheets and check your budget. It's essential that these are all accurate, so you can track your spending and profits. They will also advise you on how you can minimise your tax burden by telling you what is tax deductible. You need to know this when you start, because it will affect the amount of money you are left with after all your outgoings. Make sure you keep a constant track of your earnings and expenses, even if they seem small to start with. Remember that you are eventually going to have to pay tax so make sure you are keeping enough money aside for when the tax office calls.

You will almost certainly need a web presence. But you might not necessarily need to spend a fortune at first. I know of some successful start-ups by therapists who have got by initially with just a Facebook page. If you are happy with writing for the web, or have any marketing background then a cost-effective option might be to choose one of the standard web-building packages from companies such as Vistaprint or Yola. These allow you to set up a site without having to do any coding. They have a great advantage as you can change your site as often as you want. The disadvantage is they are not as flexible or as distinctive as a bespoke option.

You will need professional indemnity insurance. Your professional organisation will be able to advise you on providers. Remember indemnity insurance is necessary to protect you, and its cost is tax deductible but it is also an important part of your professional image.

Once this is done you are ready to go.

Remember
A separate phone line and email address can make life simpler.

Get an accountant straight away. It will save you money later.

FIRST DAYS

Chapter Two

Prepare for your first day

Feeling nervous about your first day? You will feel better after this "dry run".

Make sure your first day is not your first day. Wherever you are working, in your home, a new office, or part of a therapy centre you will be much calmer and more confident if you have done a "dry run" first.

The day before you start

Go to your office (whether that is in your home, or somewhere else) at the time of day when you will have your first client in a couple of days. Then go through this checklist:

Is everything on show (books, certificates, folders) there because you want it to be there? Is it adding to your professional image? If not remove it or hide it. It is a good idea to have your qualification certificates and your professional indemnity insurance discreetly on display. It will help your clients feel confident about seeing you.

Are the chairs properly placed for that client? (You will find that you sit at different places for different clients, but you will probably have a default setting, or sitting.)

Sit in the client's chair so you can see things from his or her point of view. Does it feel comfortable, does it feel secure, and are there any distractions?

Check your equipment. If you are using headphones during the session, are they working? If you are recording the session is the recording clear? Do you have pens and paper to take notes? If you plan to print out material for your client as the session develops, then make sure your printer is working.

The "dry run". Three key steps
Now do a "dry run" – you might want a colleague or friend to act the client role.
Run through the following:

1. Arrival
The client rings the bell, answer, let the client in and welcome him or her. What exactly are you going to say?

Have your initial greeting worked out, knowing you can be spontaneous when you are more experienced and feel more confident. The more prepared you are, the more confident you will appear and that will put your clients at ease. Think about this and come up with some phrases which suit your approach and personality. Some good standbys are: 'Glad to see you got here okay.' 'Did you manage to park nearby?' 'Well done for finding it here, it is not that easy.' You will also quickly find that these seemingly trivial chats can tell you a lot about your client. I remember this exchange with a client who I knew worked at a local school from her email address.

Me: 'Hi, have you just walked up from the school then, it's not far is it?'

Client: 'No, but it is all uphill.'

Me: 'That's true. Are you a teacher at the school?'

Client: 'Do I look like a teacher?' (said in a gloomy voice).

If you plan to print out material for your client as the session develops, then make sure your printer is working.

Did this person tend to look on

24

the negative side of things and lack confidence in her own abilities? Yes she did, and I had some inkling of this from our initial few sentences.

If you are seeing clients one after the other it is a good idea to leave a bit of space between each appointment, so the clients do not meet.

2. First time in the therapy room

Once in your therapy room, invite the client to sit down and indicate where you want them to sit. Remember the client may well be very nervous and not know at all what to expect, so you need to guide them. Check that the client is comfortable, if they are feeling shy and nervous they may not tell you. Ask if they are too hot or too cold, tell them where the toilet is.

As the client is settling down you can begin to tell a bit about your therapy and what is likely to happen in the session.

Once the client is comfortable, ask if they are ready to start.

This serves two purposes: firstly it puts the client in an active relationship to their therapy; secondly it takes the interaction between the two of you to the therapist/client stage. You are signalling that the important work is about to begin.

Next you will need to explain your terms and conditions and work with the client to complete your information form (go to www.firstdays.co.uk to download an example). Never skip explaining the terms and conditions – it will help focus the client's attention, it will show that you are a serious therapist not some oddball, and it will cover both you and the client if there are any future problems. At this point you should also explain your fee structure and take any money.

Ask the client to turn off their mobile phone. And then go into the session.

3. Ending the session

Aim to end the formal therapy part of the session about 10 minutes before the client will expect to leave. This gives the client time to process what has happened before they go out into the outside world and gives you time to listen to their feedback. Some clients will want to tell you all about it, others will be more reticent. You do not necessarily need to read anything into this, some clients will take time to come to a view of how they find the therapy.

When the client is ready, (that is back and focused on everyday world) book another appointment with the client if this is wanted. Often they will ask your advice on when they should come and see you again. Give them an appointment card, even if they record the appointment in their phone.

Your appointment card will have your company name and contact details so it is another marketing tool. It is also a good idea at this time to reiterate your cancellation policy (go to www.firstdays.co.uk for an example). Short notice cancellations, or even worse clients just not showing up, are costly and disruptive, so keeping them to a minimum is important. In addition, spelling out this policy will encourage your clients to take you seriously as a professional whose time is valuable.

See the client out. Remember to leave enough time between your appointments. You don't want different clients meeting in the doorway if you can avoid it.

Remember
If you check everything you will feel more relaxed and the session will go better.

The client will not know what to expect. Put yourself in his or her place. What would you want to know?

Chapter Three

Admin can be made easy

Make sure all your systems can be scaled up as you get busier.

When you are seeing lots of clients, you will be glad you started slowly. Don't believe it? Well, think of it this way. Take a look at all the processes you need to do every day to ensure you serve your clients well and run your business efficiently.

Then ask yourself if you could manage these processes properly if you had twice as many clients, five times, 10 times? See what I mean?

You need to make sure your processes are smooth, efficient and as easy as possible before you even start seeing clients.

Your appointment diary

Perhaps you have started off with a paper diary. This may be best for you but it is worth considering using an electronic diary. If you use a program like Microsoft Outlook, you can do the following:

• See at a glance a full record of a client's appointments – previous and up-and-coming.

• Email your clients a meeting invitation so both of you have an electronic record of the next appointment.

• See at a glance how your diary looks for the next month or even the next year.

Another option is an online booking system which you can install on your website. Clients accessing your website can see your availability and book directly, without having to phone you. This will certainly save you time, but it does have a downside. Many therapists prefer to talk to their clients before they book and to advise and guide them on frequency of appointments, or even best times of the day to come.

Whichever system you choose make sure you back it up. If you keep a paper diary keep a copy – if you go electronic, back it up to a hard drive and keep that drive secure and separate, with a password. Then you will not need to have any sleepless nights worrying about how you would cope if you didn't know which clients were due to see you today. Scary when you think about this isn't it?

Alerts and reminders

No-show clients are a bane of the therapist's life. But there is something even worse waiting for you out there. It will happen sooner or later, but you can minimise the risk. I refer to that dreaded day when two clients turn up at once for the same appointment.

If you have emailed a meeting invitation/appointment as suggested above you will have cut down the risk. But this might have been some time ago and people can get muddled (perhaps even you!). So the day before the client is due contact them to remind them of their appointment. Increasingly, I do this by text as most people have their mobile phone with them at all times, while their email might only be accessible at work or their computer may be down.

My standard text alert to a client says:

'Hi (name) Hope you are doing fine and just a quick reminder that we have an appointment at (time and date) Best wishes Ann from Wellthought Talking Therapies.'

I keep this stored in the draft messages in my phone and can just add the details for each client. Quick and easy. An alert has several benefits, both practical and therapeutic.

On the therapeutic side, it will concentrate the client's mind on the forthcoming appointment; this gives them a chance to reflect on progress they have made. If they lack confidence, as many clients do, they may have a pleasant surprise when they reflect and find they have achieved more than they thought they would. They will also have time to think about how they want the next session to go. This will increase their participation in their own therapy, increase their sense of ownership and empowerment and that means their therapy with you is more likely to succeed.

On the practical side: it will remind them when their appointment is, it will ensure they know the exact time. And it should show up any confusion or mistakes which could have led to that dreaded two clients at once problem.

All that for the sake of a short text message. It's worth it.

Your basic information form
You need a set of basic information before you first begin therapy with a client. So what do you need and why?

Obviously the name, then the address. The address can tell you a lot, what sort of area the client lives in, how far are they travelling to see you. (You can download a copy of mine at www.firstdays.co.uk)

Next comes date of birth; it is often helpful to know how old your client is and getting their date of birth means you can keep in contact with them through the years by sending them birthday greetings if that seems appropriate.

Ask the client's gender: if they are filling the form online it might not be obvious from their name. Also, they might be transgender and this enquiry might elicit this.

Then you will need the client's phone number.

Make sure you ask if it is okay to call on that number: double check this as clients can say yes without thinking it through. If they give you a landline number, ask if they are happy for other people who may pick up the phone to know they are seeing you. If they give you a mobile, ask if another person ever checks it and is that okay?

It is important to get a client's personal email; you may wish to send the client documents and web links, with their permission. Then ask their occupation, as this will tell you a lot. Just for starters you will get an idea of the client's likely income and educational level, whether they work shifts, whether they are on a career ladder and how secure their job is.

Next comes the reason they are coming for therapy. This is pretty obvious really, but remember what a client thinks they need help with might not be the thing they really need help with.

You may find as you see them and they begin to trust you and open up to you that the real concern lies elsewhere. However, it is useful for some clients to have a little time on their own to reflect as to why they think you can help. This is also a time for you to find out if your client has unrealistic expectations as to what you can do for them. For example, if a client says: 'I want to lose weight without any effort,' then you have some straight talking to do.

Then ask if they have received any other treatment for this issue. This gives you a chance to see how long they have struggled with a concern or trouble and what has worked or not for them.

Remember in the first session to ask the solution-focused question: 'What has changed for you that you would like to continue and develop since you first made this appointment.'

Ask the client if they are they receiving any medical or psychological treatment at the moment and if they are taking any medication? This might reveal underlying conditions, including conditions which would preclude you treating them. It may also be they are seeing another therapist at the same time as you. You will then need to decide whether you can happily work with this.

Then ask how long they have been receiving this treatment. This may give you an idea of whether the treatment they are receiving is working.

Ask the name and address of the doctor of your client (and the client's permission to contact the doctor). In many circumstances it will be appropriate to write to the doctor to say what you are treating the client for and your general approach. It is also a

Ask if they have received any other treatment for this issue

useful way of getting your name known around the local health and clinical community.

Keeping good case notes

This is a professional as well as a business responsibility. You must do it, so make sure you get the most out of it.

Firstly, get into a good routine which suits you. My preferred option is to leave enough space between appointments to write up my notes. This has two advantages: that space can, in an emergency, be used to overrun an appointment (if a client is very distressed, for example). More routinely, I find notes are easier and quicker to write and of a higher quality the nearer to the time you actually saw the client. But whatever you choose, time how long it takes you and then set aside that time as often as you need. Your case notes should cover:

- Identification of client
- Date and time of appointment (s)
- Progress since the previous appointment and any contacts between appointments
- Treatments and interventions
- Your observations about the client
- Any homework or support materials you have given them
- The client's assessment or rating of the session
- Thoughts and ideas for the next session or follow-up
- Date of their next appointment
- Amount they have paid you and method of payment.

If you lay this out as a table you will be able to see this all at a glance. (Go to www.firstdays.co.uk to download a copy) Getting this right for you takes some trial and error. If you are just starting to see clients (even if it is just friends and relatives at the moment) take good notes of the work you have done with them.

Put the notes away and return to them several weeks later. Ask if your notes are telling you everything you need to know? Are they too bland and impersonal? Are they too personal, are your feelings obscuring what happened? Adjust as seems appropriate for you.

Remember you must keep within the Data Protection Act with all your records. Your professional organisation should be able to advise you on how to do this safely.

Then make sure everything is in sync. Use case notes to record every contact you have with your client. Keeping a record of every client contact is becoming more important as we find more and more ways to communicate. You need somewhere (and case notes is the place) to record every contact whether it is text, mobile, landline, email or Skype as well as face-to-face. Don't make the mistake of believing you will remember whether you emailed or texted the client, when you have a full client list you won't. Refer to these notes just before the next session to refresh your memory. Keep your case notes and files secure.

Other useful paper

Keep a pile of printed receipts for payment, number them sequentially, and date them as you use them. Alternatively, you might just purchase a receipt book. If you have a scanner, you might want to scan each one before giving it to the client. If not, then make sure you record the number, date and amount on the receipt.

Keep some standard invoices for your professional expenses.

Keep a price list handy. You might even choose to display this in your therapy room. For many clients how much they are going to end up paying can be a source of anxiety. So showing them the price list can help them feel calmer and more in control.

Compliment slips can be useful to pop in with any other information you are giving a client. It is one more way of keeping your name, phone number and website in the client's mind.

Feedback from clients is very important. It will help you gain more insight into what works and what does not. It may also be very important for your wider profession, as complementary and talking therapies become more accepted by mainstream health services there is a growing demand for evidence of their efficacy and your evaluation forms may help with that.

Do remember though to get each client's written permission if you plan to use their feedback in any study or research. A standard evaluation form will cover:

• What the client came to see you for
• What they felt was positive about the experience (on a numbered scale)
• How satisfied they were with their treatment
• Would they recommend the treatment to a friend or relative with the same problem?
• Would they come back in the future?
• Any other comments

There are a number of admin type things which you will need to master and keep which your clients will never see, but they are necessary to make your business run more smoothly. So make sure you have any passwords you need kept safely and securely (and remember to password protect all your client records). Keep safe and near-to-hand any log-ins to your own website and any other websites you use or contribute to and store in your favourites or bookmarks the URLs to the websites you use most frequently. You will need to keep a stock of basic stationery. Work out how many of each form, leaflet, and business card you will need if you achieve the maximum number of clients you want to see for the next six months, then order this amount as you will get a discount on the bulk. Don't order for more then six months as you may want to adjust as time goes by.

Remember
Time spent keeping good records will save you time later on.

Your basic information form will set the scene, showing your client that you are a serious professional.

Chapter Four

Your first clients

It can seem difficult to find clients at first so be patient and persistent.

If you are quiet at first, then use this time well. Getting clients takes focus and effort, so you need to make a plan of action.

Your first task will be to get yourself as well known in your area as possible. Start with what you know. Some people start by asking friends and neighbours if they would like help and perhaps see them at a reduced rate. If you do this, then get in a certain frame of mind. You might not be getting much money, but you can get much of value in experience and practice. You're now running a business; if you are going to be successful you need to take yourself seriously right from the beginning. So spell it out. I will see you, it will be good for me to get more practice and experience: can you reciprocate in some way?

Here is an example. If you are treating a friend for a reduced rate you will know where that friend works. Will your friend take some leaflets advertising a special introductory offer from you into his workplace? Then be detailed, don't just say: 'would you mind taking these leaflets into your office?' Say, 'I have 100 leaflets here, can you take them around three departments and put copies on ten notice boards around the building?'

If you have a few friends like this, you can build up a presence in many local workplaces very quickly.

Offer to do free sessions for people who have influence in your locality. This could be local newspaper journalists, people who own or work in businesses and shops in your local high street, or people who are well known for working in the local community in neighbourhood groups and campaigns.

Use who you are. What are your interests and expertise? Who do you know? Think about how you can use things you do in your everyday non-work life to help build your business. For example, if you play a sport can you offer motivation sessions for fellow members of your team?

If that goes well then you can build upon this. Would it make a good story for your local newspaper? Can you offer the same service to a local league? And don't forget the one-to-one approach. If someone in your team has improved their performance since you saw them then perhaps there is something else in their life which they would like to deal with. Why not ask them?

You will find that a client who you have helped with one thing will often want to come back with another issue which has been bothering them.

Don't get disheartened if you don't get masses of phone calls from this sort of marketing at the beginning. You may find that months or even years later someone phones saying they heard about you. Keep up your marketing and it will eventually pay off. As this type of exposure is costing you so little in money terms, you only need a few successes to be making a tidy profit.

I am seeing one client at the moment who contacted me because she attended a free talk I had given at a local university three years previously. She is the third person from a group of eight who has seen me since I did that talk and two other people have come to me because they heard about this talk. Or put it another way, I have made thousands of pounds from a one hour talk. Not a bad return.

Here are some things you can do to attract clients without spending a fortune.

Ask everyone you know who works if they can put leaflets or postcards on their work notice boards or put an advert on their work Intranet. This will almost always be free so any clients you get are pure profit.

Treat friends and acquaintances for a reduced rate or even for free if they contract with you to carry out certain activities to get you more clients. Make what you require of them detailed and concrete and check up that they have done it.

Talk to local groups. Check if colleges or large local workplaces such as councils have a wellbeing week or event and offer to speak there. Contact local churches and business groups to offer to speak to meetings they might be having.

Look at local newspapers and freesheets to see if they run a local groups session. Contact any of these groups which seem suitable and offer to speak to them.

These things are simple and not costly. They take some time, but they will pay off for you.

Remember

Be patient, things you do early on may pay off much later.

Use who you are and what you do to maximise your contacts.

Chapter Five

Golden clients

Care for them and they will repay you by building your business for you.

As your practice begins to mature, however you will notice that you find some clients are easier to work with than others. This is important to how you build your business.

Finding your golden clients

With some clients you have more successful outcomes more quickly, you feel they enjoy seeing you and they appreciate your efforts. You really look forward to seeing these clients.

One warning here: don't only see clients who are "like you" – this can mean you end up losing your objectivity and begin to over-identify with your clients. But you will almost certainly find that there are some sorts of clients with whom you feel more comfortable. You may notice you have better outcomes with people of a certain age, gender, or educational level. For example, perhaps you are very good at treating people for say weight problems, but don't seem to do so well with substance abuse clients.

Keeping good notes (see www.firstdays.co.uk for a template for case notes) really matters here – as it does nearly everywhere as we will see. Do your notes show you that certain sorts of interventions work best with a certain sort of client?

If you are failing in one area, then you can decide to avoid seeing clients with that issue, or you can try out some new materials and ways of conducting your sessions, or ask your supervisor. Whichever way you go forward, your notes will help you determine what is working and what isn't. These notes are your evidence base. Use them as your guides to where and how you want to work.

Remember, success counts more than anything else you do. You feel better as a therapist if your clients are leaving your sessions functioning better. Successful clients are the ones who will tell their friends about you, clients with whom who you've failed won't; worse, they might even tell people you are no good.

You will also need to look at your clients from a business point of view if you are to build a successful, profitable business. How much do you need to earn for each client session?

This may mean you need to charge a rate which many people will not be able to afford. If it is, target your practice to those groups that can afford you. If you can work for less, then you might decide to spread your practice to groups that cannot usually afford private therapy. This can also make a good story for the local press.

Profile of the golden client

Golden clients come in all shapes and sizes, but if you come across someone with the following characteristics then celebrate. Start by looking at how your clients relate to you. Are your clients ones who:

• Are ready and willing to fully engage with the therapy.

• Understand and value the fact that therapy is a partnership between themselves as the client and you as their therapist.

• Have (or can get) the resources to make the changes they want to make.

Be fair and ethical at all times but keep in mind that you are running a business.

• Understand that successful therapy will take some time and effort on their part.

Then ask yourself how they relate to the world around them? Your golden clients will have at least some of these characteristics.
• They are good networkers.
• They are well known in your local area (if your business is locally-based and it probably will be when you start).
• They like talking about themselves and their activities. (So they will tell others about what therapy is like and what they are getting out of it).
• They have a good professional reputation (so when they tell their work colleagues or their clients or customers how good your therapy is those colleagues and customers take notice).
• They are involved in local social life; things like charities and campaigning groups. Soon they will ask you to speak to the groups they are involved with.

You will notice that clients who relate well to the world around them are often the clients who have the sort of attitude which leads to successful therapeutic outcomes. These are the people who will build your business. You will get very good feedback from these clients, if something is not working they will tell you and may ask to approach the problem in different ways. Less engaged clients may simply stop coming and you might never be exactly sure why.

With these golden clients, you can work with them and also learn from them as you are doing so. This can be a virtuous circle. You are working with clients, earning money doing what you want to do, increasing your chance of a successful outcome, and you are learning from every session.

Your golden clients will tell people they know how well their therapy is going. They love to help other people and so if you are helping them, they will love to pass on their new discovery to their friends, colleagues and acquaintances. This creates what I call "the reputation ripple", that is positive feedback spreading through your community – you cannot buy that however big your advertising budget.

This reputation ripple can and often does lead to a buzz of interest and immediate referrals. Don't get disheartened if these referrals are a trickle rather than a flood. Look at it this way, potential clients only become clients when they have a problem that needs solving and they feel they are in a place where it's time to tackle that problem, that can be months or years, but eventually they will see you.

What will be happening is the almost undetectable ripple effect as news of you begins to spread through the high value social networks your golden clients have. You will be surprised, or it may be you never know! One thing you can do though is to ask your clients how they found you. This is very important as it is the only way you can find what it is that is working to bring you new clients.

You will try to do your best for all your clients, but as you get busier keep your business head clear and don't be afraid to make choices. If you have limited extra time to give to clients (say giving them materials between sessions or making follow-up calls) then make sure you deal with your golden clients first.

Make sure you are always in the mind of your golden client.
Text the client asking them how they are doing and be prepared to respond when they tell you. This takes time, so work out the maximum commitment you can give. Be fair and ethical at all times but keep in mind that you are running a business.

Give them access to other information which you know about as a professional. Remember these clients will be engaged in their treatment and will be more than willing to read an article you found on the web or watch that YouTube video of a well-known therapist exploring the area which concerns them.

Can you keep them as a client after their initial problem is solved? If you have found something else which they would like to deal with in your sessions together then plan out some more sessions with them. Make sure you discuss with them in an open and ethical way and watch they are not becoming dependent upon you.

Also, you may consider offering them a gift or a free session for any referrals they give you.

Invite them to be Facebook friends on your professional page. Then take time to like, share and message with them. Ask to join them on LinkedIn; you might find a professional network from which you can benefit. If you do either of these things make absolutely sure that you have a professional profile separate from any personal pages. You need to keep your professional boundaries clear.

Would your clients be interested in finding out about a free demonstration of some new techniques which may help with their problem? Would they be interested in a peer support group which you can set up or even facilitate? Would they be interested in something fun: if you have some ex-smokers for example perhaps they feel so much better they want to start taking exercise, think about getting a free group session at a local gym.

If you do any of these tell people about it. It will make you look dynamic and friendly and able to make things happen. This is just the sort of person most of us would like as a therapist in fact.

Remember
Clients with a high reputation in their area will increase your reputation in yours.

Clients who are good networkers will bring you more clients.

Chapter Six

Managing difficult clients

Minimising the harm difficult clients can cause you and your business is possible.

No-one has a 100 per cent success rate with clients. And failing with a client can be bad on all sorts of levels. For them, it can feel like yet another attempt to change has ended badly. For you, it can knock your confidence as a therapist and can potentially damage your reputation.

So how do you do the best for your clients and, at the same time, protect yourself personally, professionally and as a business?

Pick your clients

Here is a story which inspired me. When I first became a hypnotherapist, I met a friend of a friend at a party who had heard what I was doing and wanted to know more.

She was a high-flying television executive by the time I met her but, she told me, as a younger woman she had been crippled with shyness and unable to follow the sort of career she wanted. She was very enthusiastic about hypnotherapy, because she attributed her confidence now to a few sessions with a hypnotherapist all those years back. The interesting thing was that she perceived that he had chosen her. Here is what she told me: 'I spoke to him on the phone, and then I had a face-to-face consultation, which he charged me for. It was quite a lot of money for me at the time in fact. At the end he said: "I think I will be able to see you." I thought what a cheek, I'm paying him. But later, when we had worked together, I saw his point. I appreciated he was being honest and professional. He wanted to be as sure as he could that he could help me before taking more of my money.'

So perhaps you can start with this same mindset. With every client you see, start with asking yourself if you have a realistic chance of being able to help this person. Does it feel right? Am I a good fit with them? Do I have the right skill-set to help?

If you are always prepared to say no to a client, referring them on to another therapist where you can, then you have much more chance of succeeding with those clients to whom you say yes.

You will get a reputation as someone who gets results and nothing comes close to that for building a successful business.

Getting clients to listen

Many clients live in a busy, buzzy world where there is too much going on and they cannot see a clear way to change. That's putting it politely; quite a few of them live in utter chaos. Often that is a big part of the reason they are sitting in your therapy room, but they might not realise this. They may well be focused on a single issue which they identify as the cause of all their misery.

So you may find someone sitting in your therapy chair who has come with a stated reason for being there, giving up smoking say, but has all sorts of other things going on. Sometimes this is fine, you can help them give up smoking and

You may decide some clients are just too draining of your precious energy for you to continue to see them.

that is wonderful and possibly it will be the start of changing other hurtful behaviours.

But sometimes the buzz of a chaotic life can be a real obstacle, even an insurmountable one.

And this can be a real problem. Every experienced therapist will have come across the client who constantly makes excuses about why they haven't listened to the recording you gave them, or filled out the thought diary or. . .not done whatever you have agreed with them. If you have one of these clients, then it may be worth discussing with them if this is an optimum time for them to embark on change or if there is another therapist with whom they could work more successfully.

Having this sort of discussion is almost always positive, but not always in the same way. You might find the client suddenly realises they need to focus and you both go on to a successful outcome. Or the client might begin to realise they find change difficult, and lack the confidence to sort out what is important to them – so you can help them with that. Some clients however will come to realise that this is not a good time for them. That is fine, they will leave you feeling you have been honest, upfront and have not deceived them or made promises you cannot keep. Those clients are very likely to come back. In the meantime they may pass on that warm feeling about you to others.

Even when you fail

If you are punctual, professional and give freely of your time then clients will like you. This sounds obvious doesn't it, but remember this applies to those difficult clients too. In fact it can be even more important in managing these clients.

Even if at the end of a programme of treatment the client hasn't succeeded (say they are still smoking); if you have given them good quality recordings, materials to help and support them between sessions and other things which you feel can benefit them, then they will feel you have done your best. They might say: 'It didn't work for me, but she was really good, she did. . . (They then tell all the great extra things you gave them).' So even "failures" can build your reputation.

Do all this and you will minimise the number of clients who are really dissatisfied. Unfortunately, if you are busy, for example if you have clients in double figures coming through your doors every week, you will get some clients you just cannot please or help.

So what do you do if a client is angry and upset with you? Never, ever get into an argument with a client. Let them speak, and then answer speaking calmly and slowly. (Remember everything you have learned about body language, be assertive but not aggressive.) If they try to interrupt you at this point ask them not to. If they do interrupt, wait until they have finished and then say you are not prepared to continue the session unless they respect you and are prepared to listen. If necessary, terminate the session.

Remember, you make the rules. You are in control and you have the professional standing to take control of the situation. If you have to terminate a session, you might consider whether you want to see this client again.

Remember, you do not have to, you deserve to be treated well and you deserve to get fulfillment out of your job. Keep this in mind and you might decide some clients are just too draining of your precious energy for you to continue to see them.

If you do decide to see a difficult client again, then you will want to consider how you recalibrate your relationship with them. Keep in mind you are taking control and trying to show the client how they can better control their own behaviour.

It is often useful to send an email. It gives the client time to reflect in private. This way, you leave the door open to the client and you maintain your professional boundaries.

Thankfully, these situations are rare, but they are upsetting and can knock your confidence, so it is worth being prepared.

At www.firstdays.co.uk you can find a template for an email you can send to such a client.

Money talks to the "no-show" clients
Get any two therapists together and eventually the talk will turn to clients who don't show up. I don't know of any research into this, but it does seem

that the talking therapies are particularly plagued by this problem, which is probably not surprising when we remember that the people who are coming to see us are not functioning at their optimum level. Still, as sympathetic as we are, the no-show client is expensive, disruptive and confidence draining. So what to do?

There are different approaches to dealing with this. Make sure you send out reminders, that way you are more likely to get the client who is not going to show up to let you know. Then you might consider making the clients pay in advance. You can do this by installing a credit card facility or a PayPal facility on your website or just asking a client to pop a cheque in the post if you take a telephone booking.

Then make it clear you will charge for the appointment if you do not receive a reasonable notice, say 48 hours, of cancellation. However, you may sometimes want to be flexible about this. If someone is ill, or has a genuine emergency then it may break any rapport you have built up with them if you implement a charging policy. But it is good to have the rules in place so you can then decide whether or not you implement them. You can find out more about how to deal with clients who don't show up in Chapter nine.

The client who expects magic
If I had a pound for every client who says 'I don't expect magic!' I would be rich. If I had a pound for every client who meant it, I would not.

This isn't an easy issue to deal with, especially if you use hypnotherapy, NLP techniques, EDMR or EFT, and some other techniques as well, I am sure.

Sometimes the progress you can make with a client does seem magical. But remember, it is a bit like a swan gliding along – it seems effortless, but the elegant creature is paddling like mad below the water. You are that elegant creature and those so called magical advances are hard won.

You have used a great deal of skill and training and don't forget that. You have helped your client to get to a state of mind where they can make the changes they need. And your client has been open-minded and brave enough to take that leap into the unknown which change always involves.

It is important to manage clients' expectations right from the beginning.

Always be on the alert for the passive voice. Clients who talk about having therapy done to them need to be gently talked around to understand that their input is absolutely necessary to the process. Often it helps to test these clients, give them things to do between sessions. If you find they haven't done what you both agreed, then challenge them. You may find all sorts of misconceptions as to how therapy works and what therapy is. Or you may find the client doesn't understand what is being asked of them, or the client understands, but does not believe they have the resources. Once you have drawn this out, you can help the client deal with it and are on the way to a successful result.

But, if you see a lot of clients, you will eventually come across someone who says: 'It hasn't worked, what are you going to do about it,' or 'I don't feel any different, I want my money back.'

Often the client's frustration and disappointment will present itself as aggression or passive misery which makes the situation even more difficult.

The first thing to do is to question the client's perception. In a great majority of cases you will find that they have made progress, they are just so used to failing that they assume the worst.

If you have worked with your client to track progress you will have the evidence to show them. Using ratings scales is a great way of getting a client to track their own progress. These do not need to be complicated – you can start by simply asking a client if they feel better after the session than before. If you are not familiar with ratings scales you can find an example at www.firstdays.co.uk. Or your professional organisation may be able to provide them.

If you are seeing a client for a specific problem over several sessions, then you should also be tracking progress for that issue. So, for example, is a client you are seeing for weight loss actually losing weight? If you are using good tracking tools (that sounds very technical, but in this case it can be as simple as making sure the client keeps a food and exercise diary and notices if their clothes are getting tighter or looser), then you will know how the client is doing at every session you see them.

You may even choose to structure sessions around the progress, or lack of it, the client is making. If they are making no progress then talk to them to find out if they are doing what you both agreed they would do to help themselves. Be flexible in your practice and think about how you can adjust what you are doing to help the client. If they are making some progress are they frustrated at the speed? Often this is a sign of that magic myth, clients expect results too quickly. Or they expect solving one issue will transform their world into a perfect heaven. So help them to be both optimistic and realistic.

Replace magic with teamwork – the team is you and the client and you are there to work together. You will not engage every client in this; some will nod and not listen. But with the vast majority you will make progress and you will be perfectly happy that you have done everything you can to help.

With this mindset, you can treat complaints that you did not do magic as information to build on rather than a judgment which you must accept.

Remember
Look after yourself, you can't please every client.

Learn to manage the client's expectations.

Chapter Seven

Selling yourself

Producing high quality materials is about telling your clients who you are and what you do.

Put yourself in the client's place. It's quite likely that they have never visited a therapist before.

Anything you can do to put them at ease, give them good information in a form which they can easily take in and show yourself in a professional light will help.

So ask yourself: "If I were the client, what would I want to know before I came for therapy?" With this in mind, you might want to put together the following materials which present you in the strongest possible light. As you are offering a personal service, you need to talk about you.

So, what does a client like to know?

Start with your background (don't be afraid to tell you clients a bit about yourself. Be chatty, it will put your potential clients at ease if they feel they know a little about you before they walk through your door.)

Next come your qualifications.

Make sure you explain these, what did you have to do to obtain this qualification and what external bodies validate it. Work on this; remember many complementary therapies are only lightly regulated. Unfortunately, this means there are a number of under-qualified and even dangerous therapists out there.

Make sure you show how different you are. Explain how you trained and what it involved. Then make it clear who is validating your qualifications.

Essentially, you are saying you are up to the job and clients who choose you can trust you.

Your niche

Then list what you specialise in. Say what you treat and what that involves. You might lose out on clients who have a problem you don't cover but you will pick up clients who are more likely to come to a therapist if they believe they have a special knowledge and experience. Collect testimonials or references, if you want to use them.

There are various ways you can go about this. One good way is to ask if you can use comments they make on your feedback or evaluation form on your website. It is generally not a good idea to use your client's full name, but if it is okay with them it can be a good idea to mention their profession. A professional musician who you have helped with stage fright, a student you have helped with exam nerves, or a teacher you have helped with workplace stress will all help you look like a serious person with serious clients who have been helped to improve their lives.

Let clients know about your membership of a professional organisation. This is another way in which you can show you are a member of a respected profession, part of a community which has rules and standards to which you adhere.

A decent professional organisation will have a good website. It should say how many members it represents, who it allows to join it, its code of conduct and ethics, and what training and continuing professional development it expects from its members.

In short, it should show that anyone who is a member is safe and qualified, that a potential client will be safe with its members. Obvious isn't it? Put a

Make sure that if you are using material from someone else you have the right to do so and credit them.

link to that website in your material.

You should also detail the length of your sessions and what extra out of session material the client can expect to receive. You can do this on the web and in print.

You can put together something simple but attractive using a simple package like Microsoft Word. If you want to illustrate your material, there are several good image libraries which offer free or very low cost photos and graphic images.

Many therapists will want to give their clients material to take away, such as recordings of the session or extra things to read. Or you might want to help your clients by encouraging them to keep journals or diaries between appointments. You will know what is appropriate for each particular client. It is worth remembering, though that these materials have a value over and above their direct therapeutic one. In addition to the direct benefit, a client will also feel that they are getting extra value for money if you give them relevant and well-produced materials to take away.

So what might this include? This will vary according to your particular therapy and your particular practice, but most therapists will find some of the list below useful.

1) A timeline, laid out in the way that reflects how you work and with an explanation of what it is. You will almost certainly discuss this with your client in session, but it can be a useful therapeutic tool for them to take away and think about in more detail.

2) An exercise diary (useful for treating clients who are suffering from anxiety, stress, or weight problems). This will help them find exercise which they enjoy and then track how often and for how long they do it.

3) Food diary (for weight loss and healthy living)

4) Alcohol diary. This is obviously useful with clients who are seeing you because they have a drink problem. However, some clients who present with other issues can be exacerbating them by drinking too much.

5) Stress diary. Often a client suffering from stress will experience a generalised feeling of unhappiness and anxiety with very little concept of where these feelings come from or how they can control them.

6) Tools for goal setting. What would your client like to achieve and what are the milestones along the journey?

7) Cycle of change, a very useful tool for assessing how ready a client is to change and where he or she is in this process. It is often a good idea to give this to the client to take away, this gives your client a chance to think and reflect further on what change involves.

8) SUDS (Subjective Units of Distress Scale). These can be useful to help a client track their progress.

Importance of branding

This is just a start list, you will want to add and adapt it to your particular practice. Whatever materials you decide upon, have them on hand so you can give them to a client if you think it will help them. It is also a good idea to keep some branded folders or wallets so you can give your clients material in a form which is marketing your brand.

So make sure you have your branding on all materials you originate.

This should include your website address and contact email and phone numbers.

Make sure that if you are using material from someone else you have the right to do so and credit them. Always credit other people's work and be aware of the legal restrictions on replicating other people's writing and work.

How to use your website and social media

There are many books and online resources on this subject and having a good online presence is becoming more and more important.

However, remember you are a therapist and not an online guru (unless you are, in which case I would encourage you to write a book on the subject!). So keep it simple, keep the costs under control, decide how much time you are going to spend on Facebook, Twitter, blogging and website building, and stick to it.

Website building and design is a business full of sharks. There are unscrupulous people out there who will use the fact that most of us have only a hazy view of how websites are developed and maintained to charge too much and to promise things which they cannot deliver.

Luckily, there are ways you can get a good deal. As with most suppliers, but even more in the world of the web, ask around.

Good sources of reliable recommendations are: the people who trained you, they will almost certainly have a website and so will have some experience of this area; people in any local business networking groups you may join; therapists in any peer group you go to; other local business people (remember, a good website editor, builder or developer does not necessarily have to have a background in or any knowledge of therapy.) You do not have to stay local, but you might want to meet the person who is going to develop your website and see them to discuss updates and improvements as you grow, so this can have advantages.

Whoever you go with, make sure you get a finite cost for the developing and hosting of the site. Then agree on a price for updating the site (think about how often you will need to update it). Next, consider if you need to build in emergency updates – say you notice a mistake has slipped through, or perhaps you are going to have to change your opening hours at short notice.

You will want to come as high up search results as possible.

For most sites, most of the time you need traffic to your site to achieve a high ranking on search engines. If any supplier offers to get you onto the first page of Google, then make sure you do not hand over any money until you see a result.

Another option is to go for a self-build site with a company such as Vistaprint or Yola. If you are okay with writing the copy for your site, this can be a cost-effective option and has the advantage that you can update it as often as you want to. Disadvantages are that the layout and design can be quite limited.

If you are going to use social media, it is important that you keep your professional and personal online lives separate. How you present yourself professionally will not be the same as how you are in your private life. It may be you don't use Facebook, for example, in your private life then that is fine, but if you do then it is worth setting up a separate page for your business.

Becoming Facebook friends with your clients can give you some really good opportunities to inform them of new products you have an offer, point them towards events, publications and other things you believe might interest them. If you post regularly in a chatty yet informative style you will build a good warm image in your clients' minds.

There is a word of warning though, you will be finding out things about your clients outside of your therapeutic relationship with them. If a client tells you in your therapy room that she has just split up with her long-term partner, you can assume she wants you to know because she believes it is important that you know this. You cannot make any of these assumptions if you read the same thing on Facebook.

Also remember your professional responsibilities do not disappear just because you are on social media. This might sound obvious, but it can be easy to make mistakes.

Remember
Keep all your material well branded and at hand.

If you are going to use social media make sure you keep your professional and personal life separate.

Chapter Eight

What will you charge?

Know your market and know your clients and you won't go wrong.

There is another hardy perennial conversation topic whenever therapists meet. Like most great conversation topics, there is not an easy answer to this, but by thinking it through you can get it right for you. So what process do you need to go through to get a pricing structure which feels right for you?

Start with the big picture. Working out what you should charge means looking inwards at yourself and outwards at your immediate environment and what the local market charges.

So let's start with the inwards. Looking inwards, means asking the simple question: 'How much do you need to earn?'

So think about your outgoings. These will include:

• The cost of your therapy room
• The cost of your website
• The cost of your marketing
• The cost of the materials you give to clients
• The cost of office supplies, computer and internet service provider
• The cost of professional insurance
• The cost of your membership subscription to your professional association
• The cost of books and other professional materials
• The cost of supervision
• The cost of continuing professional development
• Your living expenses outside of work

These are pretty basic. It's hard to see how you can do business without getting these things in place. Also remember that many of these things will be ongoing costs, they will be coming out of your profits year after year.

Your "nice to have" list

You might also want to put together a "nice to have" list. This might include a better website, more advertising or an expensive course you think would really enhance your practice. So when you are working out what to charge, factor these things in as well. Think about it this way: 'If I was seeing a reasonable number of clients, could I then afford to do (whatever your "nice things to have" list contains), plus make a reasonable income to live the sort of life I want?' If you can answer positively, then you are building a sustainable business.

Looking outwards at your immediate environment is the next thing you will need to do. Here are some of the sort of things you could be considering.

You might want to keep the costs of your initial consultation low to allow potential clients a low-risk option to see if your therapy is for them. When clients come for their initial consultation you are helping them, you are also selling your services to them. So work out how you are going to convince your potential client to pay your prices.

If you are offering an initial consultation at a lower price explain what you are going to be doing. How long will the session last? What will happen? How will this address the particular issue the client has? Put the client in charge, this session is allowing them to decide if your therapy is what they need at this time.

Another useful option is to offer discounts if the client books a series of sessions. If you go down this route you may want to devise a number of treatment packages to offer to clients. If you offer, say three, or six, or ten, or 12 sessions you can offer an incremental

If you can answer positively, then you are building a sustainable business.

discount on each of them; the more sessions the client books, the bigger the discount they get. Of course, if you go down this route be sure that you are behaving ethically. You do not want end up encouraging clients to book more sessions than they need, indeed it would be wrong to do so.

On the other hand, most experienced therapists will have seen clients who might have benefitted more if they had attended more sessions. If you are giving a substantial discount then it is important you make sure that you get the full price up front, otherwise you risk the client taking the reduced cost sessions and then walking away half way through.

If you are offering session packages to clients, then spell this out in your terms and conditions and explain that reduced fee packages are non-refundable. It is a good idea to offer flexibility as well. Tell clients that you will try your best to reschedule if they need to cancel. Reassure the client that if they find themselves in a position where they cannot continue the treatment they can suspend and rebook at a later date, however far in the future that is. That way you are being fair, transparent and ethical while ensuring that you get the benefits of selling sessions in this way.

Be confident when you are explaining your pricing to clients. Begin by convincing yourself that you are worth what you are charging. When you are explaining your pricing to clients make sure you are clear about exactly what you are providing. This not only makes it more likely that they will book with you; it will also build the client's confidence in you and what you are offering. On top of that, if the client knows what to expect, they are more likely to be relaxed and at ease when they arrive for their first session.

This is what I say:

'Our initial consultation will last for one hour, during this time we will chat together to work out how we can overcome your issue. I will give you honest and complete answers to any questions you may have. I will also tell you how many sessions you are likely to need to deal with this. I will then give you a short session of hypnosis to relax you and send you away feeling good. You will get a good idea if this therapy is for you.

If you decide you do want to see me then my standard sessions last between 60-90 minutes. I usually begin these sessions by discussing how you have been getting on since we last met and then you will have a session of hypnotherapy to help you deal with your particular problem. I will usually give you some materials to help you between sessions; after all I want to make you independent and able to look after yourself. This homework might be an audio session, or I might teach you self hypnosis. Sometimes I will ask you to keep a diary to track your thoughts and habits in the area which is worrying you – seeing when you think or behave in a way you want to change can be half the battle.

   If we decide you need more than a few sessions then you can book in advance and save on fees.'

Remember
Add up your outgoings. And note what are going to be ongoing costs.

Think about offering discounts if clients book a series of sessions.

Chapter Nine

Protecting your time

This will mean you have more time to give to clients you can help.

I am sure you look forward to calls from potential clients, but how long should you spend on the phone? There are the clients who seem very cautious about booking. They will want to know a lot about you, what you do, how you work, and then they will often tell you in detail about their problem and ask your advice. To some extent this is okay; actually it is more than okay; it is just what you would expect a serious client to do.

They are spending their money and their time and putting their mental wellbeing in your hands, so they have a right to ask lots of questions and check that you are the right therapist for them.

Many potential clients like this will turn out to be your best clients. They are serious about their treatment and have enough confidence to check and to choose what is best for them. This is good, it shows a client who is going to take an active part in their treatment and that is always helpful. There are some clients who go beyond this though. You can then find you are drifting into giving away your time and your skills for free.

There are very few times I have ever felt used or exploited in this line of work, but one sticks in my mind. I was about three months into my practice and getting busier, but still at the point where the phone ringing was an exciting novelty.

Your boundaries
A lady phoned me and asked if I could help her as she said she was suffering from a lack of confidence and finding it hard to cope with work. 'Tell me a

little more,' I said, 'the therapies I use work very well to develop confidence, so I might well be able to help.' The lady then told me in great detail, for over half an hour, about her workplace problems. I tried to direct her several times in the conversation to the therapy, to booking an appointment, to coming to see me, but with little success. I just could not stop the stream of anguish, misery and anger she felt. After half an hour, I asked her name. 'You don't need to know that,' she said, 'I'm ringing all the therapists in the area and then I'll choose.' I later found out she had phoned other therapists, from different disciplines doing the same thing.

I felt that this crossed a line. I had spent longer than I wanted to or had time for and had the strong feeling I had been a free ear for half an hour.

Fine if that had been my choice, and it often is, but on this occasion it didn't feel like that. I took some time to reflect on this, I spoke about it to colleagues and discussed it with my supervisor and learned a lot. Be clear about how much time you have. Be clear that the point of the conversation is to enable the potential client to decide if they want to embark on a course of paid treatment with you.

Establish if the potential client can, with your kindness, help and support, develop the level of trust in you as a therapist which is essential for successful treatment and a good outcome.

Lessons

First of all, do not pick up the phone if you do not have some time to talk. You will gain nothing and the potential client will feel you are not interested in them. If you are pushed for time it is much better to let the client leave a message.

When you do answer, almost always a client calling will ask: "Do you see people with xxxx." I

Make it clear that the point of this is for you both to find out if there is the potential for a successful course of treatment.

reply either 'no' (and then do my best to refer the potential client to a therapist with the relevant interests and experience) or, if I do feel I have the knowledge and expertise to help I say: 'Yes, I do. I've got a few minutes before my next client, so I can have a quick chat with you now so you can decide if you would like to come and see me. So, I'm Ann and you are. . .?'

There is no blueprint for the rest of the conversation; it will depend on the needs and the personality of the client. But keep this in mind: you have a short time to transmit and receive all the information which will lead to a hopefully successful therapeutic intervention. So using this transmit and receive idea, what can we say?

Transmit and receive

Ask the potential client enough to be reasonably sure that treating him or her would fall within your competence (you can never be really sure until you meet the potential client, but you can get a good idea).

Check that they live near enough to see you (or have the facilities to Skype if you offer this service).

Ask if the potential client can make your opening hours.

Be clear about your fees, since there is no point in spending ages talking to a potential client if they can't afford to see you. (Perhaps you offer reduced rates or even some free sessions, in which case you can keep this in mind).

Tell the client your experience and suitability to treat the particular issue the client is presenting to you. If you have seen a lot of clients with the same or a similar problem say so. You may find that, without compromising the confidentiality of your existing or past clients, you can at this point give some idea of the sort of outcomes you have had.

Explain what sort of treatment you are likely to offer the client. You may not want to commit yourself to too much detail until you have had a proper exploratory session with the client and you can say this while still suggesting the sort of things you might be doing.

State how many sessions the potential client is likely to need for their particular issue.

This will give the client some idea of the commitment they need to make in time and in money if they are serious about a successful outcome. Opening up this discussion early in your relationship with the client will enable you to begin to seed the idea that they will need to make a commitment to you as well.

Keep a checklist by your telephone and in your conversation make sure you have covered all these things.

Also keep an eye on the time. If you have decided that you will allow, say 10 minutes for these initial conversations then stick to it. (There may be a few instances when you decide to overrun, say if the potential client is very distressed, but they should be very few.). If at the end of 10 minutes you decide you can help the potential client, you can draw the conversation to a close by saying: 'I hate to cut you short but I have to get back to my clients. It feels to me we have made a very good start, if you feel that too, then would you like to book an appointment?'

If the potential client is hesitant, then allow a space for them to contact you again.

If you offer a free telephone consultation, then this is the time to say so. Don't just drift into a longer conversation by accident.

If you have time you can offer a potential client this free consultation now. Make it clear that the point of this is for you both to find out if there is the potential for a successful course of treatment. And make sure they know that you are prepared to do this because it will enable them to make the decision to commit to treatment.

Dealing with cancellations

We have already touched on this earlier in the book. It is no surprise that it needs covering twice as it is a major problem of the busy therapist.

Once the potential client has been turned into an actual client you will have to deal with the problem of clients who do not turn up for their appointments, and who cancel appointments at short notice.

It is sad, but many clients do not seem to understand how disruptive and costly this is for therapists.

Why this is, I am not sure. It might be there is a culture in the United

Kingdom of not taking appointments seriously, witness the huge number of appointments with the GP which are missed every year. Then we have to face the fact that as therapists we are usually dealing with people who are not operating at their optimum level, and this can mean they find it difficult to maintain routine and stick to goals – and this unfortunately includes your appointments.

Some therapists operate a very strict regime where they charge people for non-appearance at appointments or for cancelling with less than 24 or even 48 hours notice. The point of doing this is clear, to act as a deterrent and get clients to take their therapy seriously. Many therapists will argue that this is not just a commercial decision, it is a therapeutic one as well. If your clients take seriously their responsibility to turn up, then they are more likely to take seriously their responsibility to engage with their therapy.

All this is true, but be prepared for a poor reaction from some of your clients if you enforce this. Here is an example from my practice.

Client (two hours before the appointment), texts me, 'Sorry its short notice but I am unable to keep my 4pm appointment today,' I try to phone the client but it goes straight to voicemail so I text 'thanks for letting me know but I am afraid at this short notice I will have to charge you for the appointment.' She replies: 'Oh, if that is your attitude I won't be coming again.'

Every busy therapist will have stories like this. My take on it is that there are two conflicting world views clashing here and they are very difficult to reconcile. On the one hand there is you, the therapist, with a limited amount of time organising a professional diary and juggling different clients and other professional demands.

On the other there is a client who may well be quite disorganised, even chaotic in other areas of their life and just not used to having to plan and stick to a plan.

They see any attempt by you to penalise them for this behaviour (changing their appointments or not turning up) as you being unsympathetic, harsh and acting in a way they do not expect a therapist to act.

My experience is that most clients who cancel, offer reasons for doing so and these may well reflect difficult lives. Children not being picked up by a partner, unscheduled overtime at work and family sickness are all common reasons given.

One client I had cancelled appointments no less than 14 times in a period of three months. As I had seen her for quite a while before this string, I was prepared to persevere.

I knew she was having a very difficult time and when she eventually turned up, it became clear just how awful her situation was: a family death, another serious family illness, close family members divorcing and the arrest for a serious crime of another close relative had all happened in a short period. I was so pleased I hadn't done what I had been tempted to do: contact this client and say that I could not see her any more because of her constant cancellations of appointments.

Having said this, your time is precious and every client who doesn't show up is costing you money. So how can you be on the alert for the no-show client and how do you minimise the risk?

Well, first of all put your cancellation policy in your terms and conditions and take time to explain to clients that it is very inconvenient and costly for you if they don't turn up so can they please make every effort to attend their appointments.

Then text them the day before the appointment to remind them and perhaps even ask them to confirm.

Some therapists work on a pay in advance system. This is how to do it. Give an initial consultation for free, then at the end of this if a client wants to book they pay for the future appointment, at that appointment they pay for the one after that.

A therapist I know is very happy with this system and explains it to his clients as necessary because he had so many clients failing to turn up and in a therapy room with high overheads he had to do something to protect his business.

However, he does say that he has run into some sticky situations when a client who has prepaid rings two hours before the appointment to say they can't make it. Most of the time, he tells me, he just reschedules. But he believes it does help as a deterrent, and his no-show rate has greatly declined since he introduced this system.

Another increasingly popular option is to get clients to pay in advance by PayPal. This can often be made an attractive option to the client. Offer a small discount if people book and pay online. You will of course have to enable this option on your website and sign up with PayPal or a similar service, so there is a choice for you to make as to whether this is worth it. This will still leave you with a decision to make when the client contacts you asking to change their prepaid appointment at very short notice or when they expect that if they don't turn up for an appointment you will reorganise at no cost to them.

But if none of this works, and in some cases it will not, then you might want to take firmer action. So before you begin let's consider the consequences of your actions.

What are the possible outcomes of telling the client that you are going to charge them for late cancellations or not showing up? One is that they become really upset and don't turn up any more. They might even grumble about you to their friends and colleagues and this could damage your hard-won local reputation. Two, is that they pay up, but things are never quite the same again and not in a good way.

You get the feeling that they don't trust you and are less open with you. Three, is that they have a light bulb moment, they realise that your time is precious and there is a cost to you in overheads and wasted time when they do not turn up.

Then you might want to consider the possible outcomes if you just accept that some clients will behave in this way. The consequences of this course of action might be that you lose money as you still have to pay your overheads, rent, heating, a reception service and the rest, whether or not the client turns up. You may also find that if you allow a client to do this once before you know it you find they are changing every appointment and you are spending more and more time changing your diary.

You may even find that a client who behaves like this passes the message on that you are not strict about appointments and other clients begin to behave this way as well.

So out of all those possible outcomes there is only one which is really desirable, that is the client understands why they should turn up if at all possible and why they should try not to change their appointment

So whatever you decide to do about those no-shows you can aim to keep them to a minimum. What will work? Well, like all your communications with clients, start with the client. What's in it for them if they turn up for all their appointments? Do you plan out what you are going to do with your clients beyond one session? I bet you often do, so why don't you stress this to your clients?

When a client comes to you, you may well spend the first session talking to them, taking a case history, getting to the bottom of the issue. What do you do then? Plan out a series of sessions probably. At this point you could talk to the client about why you have planned things the way you have.

So, by the end of the first session with your client you will have a firm plan in place.

A plan which you will have worked out and agreed with the client. At this stage do a double check – ask the client if that feels comfortable for them. If they say, or suggest by body language that they are not completely happy then explore this until something which feels right for them is agreed upon.

Once that is agreed then double check again. Say something like: 'Right, so you are going to be coming every other Tuesday for the next three months. Does that sound okay to you? I just need to be clear with you how important it is that you attend all the sessions as we have agreed. You'll get much more out of the treatment if we spread it out in the way we agreed. Also I am very busy (you know you had to wait a little while to get in to see me), so if you don't keep appointments it can mean other people have to wait longer. So sorry to seem as if I am going on, but it makes life so much better for us both if I can be absolutely sure that the schedule we have set out is right for you.'

You can't do much more than that. Real life with all its messiness, broken routines and chaos will intervene even with the best clients. But doing something like this will help focus the minds of those clients who need a little push to respect you and your time.

Payment

When you start out the easiest thing to do is probably to take just cash and cheques with a card. Always make sure that clients know how you will accept payment before they arrive (especially if you do not take cards, as these days many people will assume you do).

Many new therapists feel embarrassed about discussing money. If you have never worked in a service role before, let alone working for yourself, it is not surprising that taking money, negotiating prices and the like takes some getting used to.

Remember that your clients will not know how to pay you, when to pay you and how it fits into the process of the therapy session. So it will make your client more comfortable if you make it clear how and when you expect them to pay.

It is generally best to take payment before the session starts. This gets it out of the way and it puts the relationship between you and your client on a firmly professional footing. It also gives you a chance to deal with the situation if the client has turned up without any money. In my experience this is a surprisingly common occurrence.

If it is a new client, do not see them if they cannot pay. It is unlikely the session will go well if you have failed to establish the proper professional relationship and that includes the exchange of money. If you live near a cash machine, then you can politely ask the client to get some money and wait for them. If this is not feasible, then politely suspend the session and rearrange.

If you do this, then it is a good idea to follow up the next day, regretting that the session had to be suspended and saying you are looking forward to the next session.

If a client who has been coming to you for some time forgets their cash on one occasion you might take the decision to carry on with the session and arrange for them to get the money to you later.

If you take this decision, it is probably best to ask them to deliver or post the money to you as soon as they get home. That way you are showing that this is not a regular occurrence and putting your client to a little inconvenience, which makes it less likely that they will forget their wallet again.

If you take cash, always make sure you have a lot of change. Work out at the beginning of each day how many clients you have and how much change you would need if every client paid you in the largest possible denomination. That is the amount of change (notes and coins) you need. This might seem a pain but it is important, nothing looks more unprofessional than scrabbling around in your bag for the odd fiver while the client looks on.

Always give the client a receipt, either on paper or delivered to their email. Do this even if they say it doesn't matter, it will avoid you ever having a dispute about money with the client.

Remember
Keep a checklist by your telephone to make sure you have asked your potential client all the relevant questions.

Keep an eye on the time when talking to a potential client. Ask yourself how much of your time you are prepared to give for free?

Chapter Ten

Use quiet times

If you learn to use these times to grow, rather than worry, you will work better.

However busy and successful you are, there will be times when the phone, doesn't ring, the clients do not come and you are alone with your thoughts.

As counter-intuitive as it might seem you should welcome these times. It is important that you make the most of them. Don't let these quiet times surprise or distress you, get used to the idea that they will occur. You might wonder if you can predict when these quiet times will come.

Actually, there are as many theories about this as there are therapists. Some people will tell you not to bother working at all in January; nobody has any money so they do not come to therapists, they will say. Others will tell you that January is a great month; the New Year means fresh starts and new resolutions. Those clients who want to give up smoking or lose weight or change jobs will want to see you as soon as the Christmas decorations are taken down.

So, say these people, January is always busy. Then there is the sunny side of the year. Take August off, you might be advised: "Everyone's on holiday or out in the sun, so you will never be busy in August." Someone else will contradict this: "People are not working so hard, they are in a more reflective mood and so they have time to deal with that problem which has always bothered them, there are always lots of clients in August."

The truth is if you are seeing clients on a one-to-one basis then you will have ups and downs at the most unexpected and unpredictable times. Even if you are very busy you are still dealing with relatively small numbers of people and this means you do not have the volume of trade to smooth out the inevitable vagaries in the numbers of people who come to see you. When you are working on your own you do not have a big pool of clients to cushion you, even if you are busy.

Look at it this way.
Say you see 10 to 20 clients a week, that's a reasonable workload: enough to keep you busy, not so heavy that you will burn out). So you are sailing on feeling very happy, the business is a success, you are in a good settled routine and then . . . you look at your diary and there is a whole day, or even two or three without any clients at all. What has happened?

Well, nothing really, as you will now have realised, you are dealing with small numbers. So a few people changing their plans can have a big impact on you.

On our 10 to 20 clients a week model, you only need 20 per cent of your expected client intake to not be around for one or another reason and you have the equivalent of a day free. Chance may mean this works out in such a way that this is one whole day at a time.

Does that mean you are a hopeless therapist? Does it mean you need to look for another line of business? No, it is just the nature of one-to-one personalised service businesses. Your hairdresser probably goes through much the same thing. But for you, as a therapist, there is an added twist and that lies in the nature of your client group.

Many of the clients who come to you are doing so because they are troubled and in some way find it difficult to organise and run their lives. Expect to be messed around to some extent and for some clients to disappear on you (the ones that do often come back later).

There are some things you can

Understanding why your days can sometimes be unpredictable is a good defence against feeling gloom and a lack of confidence.

do to minimise this disorganisation, which we dealt with in the previous chapter. Even after you have done this, like all small businesses you will have quiet times, and as we have seen, because of the particular nature of your client base you are likely to suffer more unpredictable cancellations, changes and no-shows than other people-centred businesses.

I hope that understanding why your days can sometimes be unpredictable is a good defence against feeling gloom and a lack of confidence. One important lesson I learnt from more experienced therapists when I was starting out was the golden rule "Don't worry if it is quiet, clients will appear again."

So how are you going to feel in the quiet times? It is your choice and a bit of self reflection and positive self-talk can go a long way.

Let's visualise such a day

So there you are, sitting in your therapy room, alone. What is your mindset? Are you angry, scared, bored, unhappy? At first, times like these can be frightening, this is especially true if you don't have a full client list yet. You might feel your confidence is taking a dive or even feel that you have made the wrong choice of career.

So it is important that you take care of yourself at times like this. The first thing is to make a deliberate effort not to panic. Take a deep breath and enjoy the silence . . . and rest . . . and take time to reflect. Then do the following:

Get in the right mindset. Decide you are going to enjoy this time. Look at it as a positive gift in your working life.

Say: "Good, I have time for me."

It is a useful idea to have an ongoing project which you can pick up in these quiet times. Perhaps this is your own continuing professional development.

Make a list of things you want to find out more about professionally and work you way through them. Read a book, watch a demonstration of a therapy session on YouTube, read your professional journal, do a bit of research on the web. If you do this diligently and in a positive spirit, your quiet times can lead to a published article or a new area in which to expand your practice or develop your client base. You've probably guessed what's coming next. Some of this book has been written in quiet times (although not this bit, which is being written at 7am before I start seeing clients. Knowing your best times for doing what you need to do is a good skill to acquire too).

Ask yourself: "how do I feel?" Then decide to make yourself feel better, calmer, more focused and more positive. Meditation, Emotional Freedom Technique or self hypnosis will all help. You will also be learning new useful techniques which you might want to pass on to your clients in the future.

Look after your business by marketing

This is a constant activity, so do more of it whenever you have time. Many marketing gurus will tell you the most common mistake people in small businesses make is to ignore marketing until their client list starts to shrink. To be successful, they say, you need to be marketing at all times.

You can take the opportunity to get into good habits from the beginning. You should have a marketing plan and budget, even if it is simple. There are many things you can do to raise your profile in these quiet times as we have already seen in the chapter on getting clients. So use the time to make sure you are getting your message out there to potential clients.

Another good habit you can develop is that of looking after the clients you already have and that applies even if you don't have any yet! Set up a system for keeping in contact with clients, or potential clients. You might think of producing an e-newsletter or sending a regular personalised email. If you get into the habit of keeping in contact, you will soon have a thriving business and a good reputation.

Keep up with your admin tasks. They have to be done if you are to run an efficient business and offer a timely, calm and seamless service to your clients. If you use your quiet time well, you may find that you can keep all your business systems up-to-date without having to devote any special extra time to it.

Once you have the basics sorted, then update and add to your standard materials. Even the best materials can get stale after a time. The greater variety you have at your disposal the better tailored service you can offer to each client. That will raise your rate of success and satisfied clients will spread the message. If you've done all this, you are probably stiff from sitting and bug-eyed from staring at a computer screen. So tidy your therapy room. The physical movement will do you good and you may notice some little improvements you can make to enhance your client's experience.

Stand back and reflect

Be as self-reflective as you can. Always be asking yourself, "what am I doing and how am I doing it?" Read through your client notes. Who have you seen? Analyse objectively to get a picture of the direction in which your business is going.

Are your clients a completely diverse bunch or perhaps you are building a niche seeing similar sorts of people and you haven't noticed it.

Have you seen several clients for ostensibly the same problem, but ended up doing very different things with them? Perhaps you can begin to see some patterns of what seems to suit different clients.

Stand back and look at what you have done and you will be surprised at how it is developing. Be flexible, is there a niche market you have come across you didn't expect; do you want to develop that? Be honest: are you better at some things than others? Work out how you can concentrate on what you are good at. Is there something you hate doing? If there is, what is your strategy for stopping doing it?

When you have finished looking back through your case notes you can look forward in your diary. What clients are coming to see you soon? Can you do extra preparation? Is there anything extra you would like to give them? The better their experience, the more likely they are to recommend you to others.

So, think about how to use your quiet time and build up good habits. This will pay off later and it will put you in a good frame of mind. Make sure that every minute you are working you are working. That way you will be in a continuing frame of mind to improve your performance and develop your business whatever is happening around you. These quiet times will come to seem like golden moments to you in a year or so.

Remember
Everyone has quiet times, it doesn't mean you are a failure.

Make sure that every minute you are working you are working.

Chapter 11

Second days are coming

Look after yourself, keep learning and you will sail into your second year of business.

Congratulations. If you have got this far in the book, then you know more or less everything you need to know to start your business and run it smoothly.

You will now give the impression to your clients of an experienced and competent professional.

No-one will know how new you are unless you tell them. You will exude an air of confidence and this will increase your chances of success with your clients.

So you will sail through your first year in your new business. And then into your second and third year and on for as long as you are happy to work.

Further on in your career you may find you need a bit of a reset.

Most of us find specialising in one area is beneficial to building our business. You become an expert in a field and people know you as the weightloss woman or the building confidence guy. That reputation becomes your brand and that is your most valuable asset.

You may find you are asked to write articles and give talks on your specialist area. You will attract clients who want help with the issue in which you specialise.

Keep some variety
So you are where you want to be? Well, yes, and it's great but perhaps you are beginning to feel that you need to watch out. As you are dealing with

people's problems every day it is very important that you look after yourself if you are to keep your health and happiness and also serve your clients well.

Looking after yourself is to be the subject of a follow-up book to this, but here are a few tips.

Keep some variety in your work. Even if you specialise in one area and feel happy and comfortable doing this, you can still build in some new challenges. So perhaps you can find a different type of client, perhaps you can work in a new environment. If you don't write or speak about your subject, perhaps now is the time to start.

Keep up with the latest developments in your area and make sure you meet your peers regularly. If you cannot do this face to face, then it might be possible to join an online group. Look out for webinars, discussion forums and online talks which you can join.

As you begin to be more successful you might find you have the time and resources to do some unpaid work for a charity. Make sure you choose carefully, something where your skills will be put to best use and where your expertise will be respected. Be careful to set clear boundaries and make it clear how much can be expected of you.

As you are self employed, it is very important that you keep a space between your work life and your personal life. Make sure you take plenty of time off and enjoy your time. As you are likely to be doing a fairly sedentary job, so make sure you exercise regularly.

Keep learning. It will keep you fresh and improve your practice. You may need to undertake continuing professional development as a professional requirement. This should be a minimum for your professional health and wellbeing. Choose carefully and make sure that you set aside enough time to allow new ideas to blossom and for your mind to develop.

Teach others, whether

> *As you are self employed, it is very important that you keep a space between your work life and your personal life.*

formally or informally; you will hone your thoughts by presenting them to others. It can be a very rich learning process to observe and understand how people new to your ideas interpret and understand them. It can give you a whole new framework in which to understand your practice. So good luck and enjoy learning, developing and helping as you continue in your chosen career.

Remember
Continuing professional development will help you as well as your clients.

Useful resources and websites

Professional resources

The Complementary and Natural Healthcare Council
http://www.cnhc.org.uk/
The voluntary register of complementary and natural healthcare practitioners. Packed with information to protect you and your clients. Good overview of the different disciplines in this area.

Government Gateway
http://www.gateway.gov.uk/
The place to sort out the bureaucracy associated with being self employed. (UK only registration required)

Citizens Advice
http://www.adviceguide.org.uk/england/work_e/work_self-employed_or_looking_for_work_e/self-employment_checklist.htm
A good checklist of what to do when becoming self employed

Growing a small business

http://www.smallbusiness.co.uk/
Information-packed site to help you grow a business.
http://brandingsmallbusinessfordummies.com/
No-nonsense short guide to developing an attractive brand
http://www.nickbrungerhypnotherapy.co.uk/pages/marketing-for-hypnotherapists.php
An excellent guide to marketing and practice building

VISIT MY WEBSITE

WWW.FIRSTDAYS.CO.UK
FOR THESE FREE EXTRAS (QUOTE CODE 'FIRST 14')

- Template for a reflective diary
- Client information sheet
- Sample terms and conditions (including cancellation policy)
- Template for keeping case notes
- Sample email when dealing with a challenging client
- Sample ratings scale
- Reduced cost for supervision

Index

NOTES

Printed in Great Britain
by Amazon